COOKING OF THE GULF

BAHRAIN, KUWAIT, OMAN, QATAR, SAUDI ARABIA,
UNITED ARAB EMIRATES

COOKING
OF THE GULF

BAHRAIN, KUWAIT, OMAN, QATAR, SAUDI ARABIA,
UNITED ARAB EMIRATES

Tess Mallos

PARKWAY
PUBLISHING

Contents

Introduction

While each is a separate country rather than a state, the collective grouping of the Gulf States is necessary as their cooking varies little. One can trace the origin of certain recipes to one particular place but you would also find the same dish prepared in the other countries.

The aspect of Arabic life that impresses most is their hospitality, and the single food (if it could be called such) with which this is expressed is coffee. The coffee pot is ever present, though nowadays coffee is likely to be prepared early in the day and kept hot in a vacuum flask ready for any person who comes by.

There are certain rules which should be observed if ever you are offered coffee in this region. First, do not refuse a cup: to do so is an insult to the host. Your cup will be replenished a second time and a third, and more if you do not indicate to the host that you are satisfied. A simple little jiggle of your empty cup from side to side indicates that you have had sufficient. Only a small portion of coffee is served—a third of a cup is poured each time and the handle-less cups are very small. It is always served unsweetened and flavored with cardamom. Taking two or three cups of coffee is expected of you, rather than just one; however more than three is considered impolite.

First impressions of Gulf food, particularly in the suk (market) quash any notion originally held that the staple diet was boiled meat (lamb, mutton or camel) served on a huge mound of spiced rice. While this might be true of the nomadic Bedouin, camped far from places which could provide anything else, it is not so of the food of townspeople. The variety of fresh vegetables, fruits, spices, meat, fish and poultry from which to choose would delight any serious cook and amaze at the same time, as an aerial view of the region with its vast, arid landscape does not indicate abundance, not of the edible kind anyway.

The Flavor
of Arabic Cooking

The Gulf Arabs are very fond of skewered meats, either succulent cubes of lamb similar to the kebabs of other Middle Eastern countries, or Kabab Mashwi, a meat paste moulded on flat skewers and grilled over coals. These are often served folded into khoubiz together with salad ingredients.

Their rice dishes are of the kind one would expect, knowing the colorful history of the Arabs, as it was they who opened the spice routes to India and the East, and to the West, trading their own cardamom, coriander and cumin for cinnamon, nutmeg, cassia, ginger, pepper, turmeric and cloves. The most popular spicing is a mixture of most of these, called baharat, and it is used in rice, soups, fish, poultry and meat dishes, usually with the addition of whole spices to emphasize certain flavours and turmeric or saffron for color. Often the saffron is steeped in rosewater and poured over the dish toward the end of cooking or on serving for a final dash of color and fragrance.

Shades of near-Indian cooking are to be expected with the historical links probably going even further back than those already documented. The Indus Valley civilization mysteries have yet to be unraveled, but recent archeological finds in Bahrain and elsewhere in the Gulf region revealed seals similar to those found in the Indus Valley.

Machbous is a particularly interesting dish of meat, fish, prawns or chicken cooked in spices with rice. The rice itself must be basmati as the Arab refuses any other substitute. It is an aromatic rice from Pakistan, hard of grain, which holds up to the long cooking involved. However, cooking times have been shortened in the recipes, in anticipation of possible substitutes.

One ingredient which intrigued me is the loomi (dried lime). In the Gulf region it is used extensively, either whole or pounded into a powder, and it imparts an interesting and unusual flavor to foods. It is difficult to give a substitute, but in recipes the thinly peeled or grated zest of a lemon may be used instead as a reasonable substitute. The loomi originated in Oman, where it dried naturally on the tree. Today Oman and Thailand supply the dried limes; the ripe, yellow fruit are harvested and sun-dried. I have given details in this book on how to prepare your own dried limes.

The cucumbers of the Gulf are much loved by the people and after tasting them I could understand why. The long green cucumber which we know is picked before it reaches maturity and this is when cucumbers are at their best. One other variety, a long slender cucumber with a dark green and deeply grooved skin, is available in Western countries under a variety of names. In the Gulf it is called trooh and the locals claim that when the moon is full one can hear the cucumber groaning as it twists itself into the circles and other squiggly shapes in which it comes. The English (hothouse) cucumber is a good substitute.

The waters of the Gulf teem with shrimp (prawns) and an infinite variety of fish. The most popular fish for the table are gugurfan and shehen (similar to bream), wahar (flathead), beyah (mullet), chanad (mackerel) and a popular

Kuwaiti fish called zubaidi (pomfret). Generally fish is cooked over glowing coals, oven-baked, fried or stewed.

Khoubiz is the general term for the flat breads of the area; more specifically flat bread made with white flour is called mafrooda, or mafrooda burd when made with whole wheat (wholemeal) flour. These are bubbly-textured on the surface and baked in a tannour (clay beehive oven) or a conventional bread oven. Pita bread or Indian naan are good substitutes. Samouli is another popular bread, similar to the French baguette.

Eating Arabic Style

Today the region, while still keeping its traditions, is likely to cater also to Western tastes. A town house is likely to have a living room with one part furnished with floor and wall cushions for Arabic visitors, and a table and seating for Western visitors, emphasizing the innate hospitality of the Arab.

Whether served on a cloth spread over a carpet on the floor or on a dining table, the food is presented in the same way. All the components of the meal are placed in dishes and platters, with plates, spoons, forks and glassware. Only in a Bedouin tent is one likely to have the experience of eating from a communal platter, using the fingers of the right hand.

The main dish could be meat, fish or chicken, either cooked in a rich sauce, or roasted, baked or grilled. Muhammar (a sweet rice), mashkoul (rice and onions) or muaddas (a combination of rice and lentils) is served separately unless rice is incorporated with the meat dish. A dish of fresh salad is always served, consisting of romaine (cos) lettuce, crisp firm cucumbers, tomatoes, sweet peppers, radishes and a cress-like green herb. The salad is simply dressed with vinegar. Bowls of yogurt and pickles accompany the meal and bread is always served.

If you want to serve a meal with all the exotic elements of a feast in a desert sheikh's tent, then the dish to prepare is khouzi. While khouzi is prepared throughout the Gulf States and other Arabic countries, the Saudi Arabian khouzi reigns supreme. First, you require a whole lamb including the head. A rice stuffing, redolent with nuts, onions, golden raisins (sultanas) and spices, is prepared. Some of this is packed into a chicken with shelled hard-boiled eggs; then the chicken is placed in the cavity of the lamb with the bulk of the rice mixture. The cavity is sewn up and the lamb trussed. Though frequently roasted on the spit, it is traditionally placed in a large tray with the ribs of palm leaves serving as a rack. Water is added to the tray and a lid is sealed over the tray with a flour-and-water paste. It is then oven-baked to succulent perfection. The lamb is cooked until it is so tender that the meat comes away from the bones

easily. The stuffing is removed and spread on a serving platter with the lamb resting on top.

Khouzi is served with great ceremony. Servants present pitchers and bowls for guests to wash their hands before the meal. All the components of the meal are spread on a cloth over a colorful and usually expensive carpet, with cushions scattered around. The guests sit in their places with the most important guest seated next to the host, and the host delights in selecting the most succulent pieces of lamb to offer to the principal guest. The most highly regarded parts of the lamb are the eyes and though that may repel, the Arabs consider them great delicacies. I should imagine it would be somewhat like tackling your first oyster. To serve such a feast in the traditional manner would, of course, mean that only men would be present, but this problem can be overcome by proclaiming any woman guest to be an honorary male. (There are most reputable precedents for this: the Queen of England was accorded this honor during a visit to Saudi Arabia in 1979.) At feasts of this type, eating is regarded as a serious business and there is little, if any, conversation. When the meal is finished, hands are washed again and the guests adjourn to another area for coffee or tea and conversation.

Ingredients

Basmati rice is a necessary ingredient for authentic Gulf cooking. The meat is usually lamb, but now that more food is imported, beef is gaining in popularity. Cardamom, saffron, turmeric, flat-leaf parsley, coriander, rosewater, loomi (dried lime) and dates are frequently used. Tamarind is still used in certain dishes though tomato has replaced tamarind to a great extent. A large quantity of onions should be on hand, as they are much used in Gulf cooking. The recipes and introductory chapters give more detail on Gulf foods.

ALMONDS Blanched almonds contribute crunch and subtle sweetness to pilafs, pastries and puddings.

PINE NUTS These ivory colored nuts are used in pilafs and stuffings.

PISTACHIO NUTS Their delicate flavor and color make them a favorite garnish for pastries, puddings and pilafs.

BULGUR (BURGHUL) Hulled wheat that is steamed, dried and crushed. Available in fine, medium and coarse grinds, it requires soaking before use.

CARDAMOM A spice that adds aromatic sweetness to savory and sweet dishes.

CINNAMON Bark from the cinnamon tree, dried and curled to form sticks.

CILANTRO (CORIANDER) Fragrant leaves from the coriander plant also known as fresh coriander or Chinese parsley.

CORIANDER SEEDS Seeds from the coriander plant that are dried and ground into a spice. They have a combined flavor of lemon zest and sage.

CUMIN Seeds with an aromatic earthy flavor that enhances other spices such as coriander seeds.

FLAT-LEAF PARSLEY Common parsley of the region, also known as Italian parsley.

LEFT TO RIGHT First row: Almonds, pine nuts and pistachio nuts;
bulgur (burghul); cilantro (fresh coriander). Second row: Cardamom
pods; cinnamon; coriander seeds and cumin.

BROWN LENTILS AND RED LENTILS
Brown and green lentils are unhusked. The spicy-flavored, tiny red lentils are husked.

LOOMI (DRIED LIMES) Also known as black limes. Sun-dried limes are used to add a pleasant tartness to stews and soups. Lemon zest may be substituted.

POMEGRANATE A fruit prized since ancient times for its sweet-tart juice and for its jewel like seeds. The juice is made into a syrup. The seeds are sprinkled on savory dishes and puddings.

LONG-GRAIN RICE White rice used for pilafs. Aromatic, cream–white basmati rice is preferred in the Gulf States.

MEDIUM-GRAIN RICE White rice used in stuffings for vegetables and grape vine leaves and for rice puddings.

SAFFRON The stigmas of *Crocus sativus*, picked by hand and dried in a labor-intensive process, making the final product the most expensive of spices. Possessing a pungent, aromatic flavor and intense color, saffron is available as stigmas, or threads, and ground.

SPINACH Native to Ancient Persia (Iran), spinach is a popular vegetable throughout the region, used in savory pastries and with lentils, yogurt, or eggs. The leaves can be curly or flat, depending on the season.

TAHINI A smooth, oily paste made from ground toasted sesame seeds. For the best flavor, select a light-colored tahini.

OPPOSITE PAGE, LEFT TO RIGHT First row: Flat-leaf (Italian) parsley; brown and red lentils; dried limes. Second row: Pomegranates; long grain rice; medium-grain rice; Third row: Saffron; spinach; tahini.

Sauces and Pickles

Dukkous bi tahina
Tahini sauce

Makes 1½ cups
2 cloves garlic
½ teaspoon salt, plus extra salt to taste
¾ cup (6 fl oz/185 ml) tahini
⅓ cup (3 fl oz/85 ml) cold water
⅓ cup (3 fl oz/85 ml) lemon juice

In a small bowl, crush garlic with ½ teaspoon salt and mix to a paste. Gradually add tahini, beating well with a wooden spoon.

Then alternately beat in small amounts of water and lemon juice. The water will thicken the mixture; lemon juice will thin it. Add all of lemon juice, and enough water to give sauce a thin or thick consistency, depending on use. The flavor should be tart. Add salt to taste if necessary. Use sauce as a dip with pita bread or as an accompaniment for falafel, or fried fish.

FOOD PROCESSOR METHOD Place tahini and garlic in processor bowl and process for a few seconds to crush garlic. Add lemon juice and water alternately, a small amount at a time, until desired consistency is reached. Blend in salt to taste.

VARIATION: BAKDOUNIS BI TAHINA (PARSLEY AND TAHINI SAUCE)
Follow directions for Tahini Sauce, adding 3–4 tablespoons finely chopped flat-leaf (Italian) parsley after blending ½ of water and all of lemon juice into tahini. Beat well and add more water if necessary. If using a food processor, add parsley after all other ingredients are blended and process for a few seconds. Serve as a dip or as an accompaniment to fish.

Laban bi khiyaar
Yogurt and cucumber dip

Serves 6
2 cups (16 oz/500 g) plain whole-milk yogurt
2 young green cucumbers or ½ English (hothouse) cucumber
2 teaspoons salt, plus extra salt to taste
2 cloves garlic, crushed
2–3 teaspoons dried mint, finely crushed
1–2 tablespoons olive oil
fresh mint sprigs for garnish

Peel cucumbers if necessary and cut lengthwise into quarters. Thinly slice and place in a colander. Mix in 2 teaspoons salt, and let stand for 1 hour. Shake well to remove remaining moisture.

In a bowl, combine cucumbers, yogurt, garlic and dried mint to taste. Add salt to taste if necessary.

Stir in olive oil, a small amount at a time, adding as much as is needed to make a thick, creamy mixture. Cover, chill well, and serve in a deep bowl garnished with mint sprigs. Use as a dip with crusty bread or as a sauce for fried fish, kebabs or dishes containing rice.

NOTE A thick, Greek-style yogurt is best for this recipe.

Dukkous al-Tamat

Tomato sauce

Makes about 3 cups
1 tablespoon vegetable oil
4–6 cloves garlic, crushed
1 ½ lb (750 g) ripe tomatoes, peeled and chopped
salt
1 ½ teaspoons Baharat (page 23)

Heat oil in a pan and add crushed garlic, cook only for a few seconds.

Stir in tomatoes and salt to taste. Cover and let simmer on low heat for 30 minutes. Stir in Baharat, cook with lid off for 2–3 minutes, then remove from heat. Serve with rice or as specified in recipes. Sauce may be stored in a sealed jar in the refrigerator and heated as required.

Mutabbal
Eggplant and tahini puree

Serves 4-6

**2 medium eggplants (aubergines),
each about 12 oz (350 g)**

2 cloves garlic, chopped

½ cup (6 fl oz/125 ml) tahini

4–5 tablespoons lemon juice

1½ teaspoons salt

2 tablespoons olive oil

**3 tablespoons fresh flat-leaf (Italian)
parsley, finely chopped**

Preheat oven to 425°F (220°C/
Gas 7). For a traditional smoky flavor,
prepare a charcoal fire or heat a gas
barbecue. Leave stems on eggplants
and prick eggplants several times
with a fork.

Place on middle shelf in oven or on
a grill (barbecue), and cook, turning
frequently, until soft, 30–40 minutes.
The skin should be charred if cooked
on a grill (barbecue).

Cool eggplants slightly and peel off
skin. Remove stems, chop flesh, and
place in a sieve to drain for
30 minutes.

Put drained eggplant in a food
processor bowl, add garlic, and
process to a puree. Add tahini, most
of lemon juice, salt, and olive oil and
process until light and creamy. Add
parsley and process briefly. Taste, and
add remaining lemon juice if
necessary.

Place in a shallow dish and serve
with pita bread as an appetizer.

NOTE If making puree ahead of time,
store in a sealed container in the
refrigerator. Allow to reach room
temperature before serving.

Hummus bi tahina

Chickpea and sesame puree

Makes about 3 cups
1 cup (6 oz/180 g) dried chickpeas
   (garbanzo beans)
3 cups (24 fl oz/750 ml) water
1½ teaspoons salt, plus extra salt
   to taste
⅓ cup (3 fl oz/85 ml) tahini

½ cup (4 fl oz/125 ml) lemon juice
2 cloves garlic, crushed
FOR GARNISH
1 tablespoon olive oil
fresh flat-leaf (Italian) parsley, chopped
paprika or cayenne pepper

Put chickpeas in a bowl, add water, and soak in a cool place for 12 hours or overnight. Drain and rinse well.

Place chickpeas in a saucepan with fresh water to cover. Bring to a boil, cover, and cook over low heat for 1 hour. Add 1 teaspoon salt and cook until very tender, about 30 minutes longer. Drain, and reserve some cooking liquid and 1 tablespoon chickpeas.

Press chickpeas through a sieve or food mill into a bowl, adding about 2 tablespoons cooking liquid to separate last of peas from their skins.

Slowly blend tahini and most of lemon juice into chickpea puree.

In a bowl, crush garlic with ½ teaspoon salt and mix to a paste. Stir into puree. Adjust flavor and consistency with remaining lemon juice or cooking liquid, and add salt if necessary. Hummus should be thick and smooth.

Spread puree in a shallow serving dish, swirling with back of a spoon. Drizzle olive oil in center and garnish with reserved chickpeas, chopped parsley and a sprinkling of paprika or cayenne pepper.

Loomi
Dried limes

small fresh limes, preferably Persian limes
salted water

If limes are very large, they can be halved to speed the drying process.

Put limes in a pan of boiling water with about 1 tablespoon salt. Return to a boil, and boil rapidly for 3–5 minutes, depending on size. Drain.

Place on a mesh metal cake rack and place in the sun to dry. This takes up to a week, depending on strength of sun. Turn daily. Alternatively, place rack with limes in a very low oven, set on lowest possible heat. Put in coolest part of oven and leave for 3–4 days. A warming drawer would be even better, or, if you can

get one, use an electric food dehydrator and follow the manufacturer's instructions.

Limes are ready when they are dark and the flesh completely dehydrated. Take care not to make them too dark. Store in an airtight container.

To powder loomi: Pound in a mortar with pestle or process in blender. A sprinkling of powdered loomi does wonders for steaks—rub in before broiling (grilling) or pan frying.

NOTE Thinly peeled or grated lemon zest may be used as a substitute. Remove zest in strips with a vegetable peeler as a substitute for whole dried lime; or grate zest for powdered lime.

Achar tamat
Pickled tomatoes

Makes about 6 cups
2 lb (1 kg) firm, ripe tomatoes
¼ cup (2 oz/60 g) coarse pickling salt
3 teaspoons black pepper, freshly ground

3 teaspoons paprika
2 teaspoons ground coriander seeds
6 cloves garlic, halved
3 cups (24 fl oz/750 ml) white vinegar

Choose small or medium-sized tomatoes with no sign of decay. Wash well.

Slit tomatoes almost halfway through at stem end and fill slits with salt. Place upright in a bowl and leave for 3 days. Drain off liquid as it accumulates. Invert tomatoes in a colander and leave until excess liquid drains off.

In a bowl, combine pepper, paprika, and coriander and sprinkle about ½ teaspoon of mixture into each tomato.

Pack tomatoes into sterilized jars, adding pieces of garlic between layers. Fill jars with vinegar and seal with glass or plastic lids. Leave for 1 week before opening. Use pickles within 6 weeks.

Baharat using ground spices

Makes about 1½ cups
4 tablespoons ground black peppercorns
2 tablespoons ground coriander seeds
2 tablespoons ground cinnamon

2 tablespoons ground cloves
3 tablespoons ground cumin
1 teaspoon ground cardamom
4 teaspoons ground nutmeg
4 tablespoons paprika

Purchase the freshest possible ground spices. Combine and store in a tightly sealed jar in a cool, dark place. Use within 6 months.

NOTE Baharat is available in Middle Eastern markets and specialty spice stores.

Rice, Salad and Vegetables

Ruz bukhari
Saffron rice

Serves 5–6

2 cups (14 oz/440 g) basmati rice

½ teaspoon saffron threads

2 tablespoons rosewater

5 tablespoons (3 oz/90 g) ghee or
⅓ cup (3 fl oz/90 ml) vegetable oil

¼ cup (1 oz/30 g) blanched almonds,
halved

1 medium yellow (brown) onion, finely
chopped

8 oz (250 g) ground (minced) lamb or
beef

½ teaspoon Baharat (page 23) or
ground allspice

½ teaspoon salt, plus extra salt to taste

¼ cup (1½ oz/45 g) golden raisins
(sultanas)

3 cups (24 fl oz/750 ml) chicken stock

Place rice in a fine-mesh sieve and rinse under cold running water until water runs clear. Place in a bowl, add cold water to cover and let soak for 30 minutes.

Place saffron in a mortar and pound with a pestle. Place in a small bowl, add rosewater and set aside to steep.

In a frying pan over medium–low heat, heat 2½ tablespoons ghee or oil. Add almonds and fry until golden, about 5 minutes. Remove to a plate with a slotted spoon.

Add onion to the same pan and fry until translucent, about 7 minutes. Raise heat to medium–high and add lamb or beef. Cook, stirring often, until the meat is crumbly and juices evaporate, about 10 minutes. Stir in Baharat or allspice, ½ teaspoon salt, and raisins and fry for 1 minute longer. Remove from heat, cover and set aside.

In a deep, heavy saucepan over high heat, heat remaining 2½ tablespoons ghee or oil. Add 2 teaspoons saffron mixture and chicken stock. Bring to a boil.

Drain rice and add to boiling stock with salt to taste. Bring to a boil, stirring

occasionally, then reduce heat to low. Cover pan tightly and cook until rice is just tender, about 20 minutes.

Fold meat mixture gently through rice, place a kitchen towel or two paper towels over rim of pan, replace lid and continue to cook over low heat for 5 minutes. Remove from heat and let rice stand for 5 minutes before serving.

Spoon rice into a serving dish or onto a platter. Sprinkle with fried almonds and remainder of saffron mixture. This rice is excellent served with roasted chicken or lamb, or as part of a buffet.

Muhammar
Sweet rice

Serves 5–6
¼ teaspoon saffron threads
3 cardamom pods, cracked
2 tablespoons rosewater
2 cups (14 oz/440 g) basmati rice
6 cups (48 fl oz/1.5 L) water
1 tablespoon salt
⅓–½ cup (3-4 oz/90-125 g) granulated sugar or honey
¼ cup (2 oz/60 g) ghee or butter

Place saffron and cardamom in rosewater and put aside to steep.

Place rice in a fine-mesh sieve and rinse under cold running water until water runs clear. Drain well.

In a heavy pan, bring water to a boil then add salt and rice and stir occasionally until water returns to a boil. Leave uncovered and boil for 8 minutes. Drain in a colander.

Pour sugar or honey onto hot rice and mix through with a fork.

In pan in which rice was cooked, heat ghee or butter and then stir in sugared rice. Sprinkle rosewater mixture on top. Make 3 holes in rice with end of a wooden spoon.

Cover rim of pan with a paper towel and place lid on tightly. Cook rice over low heat until tender, 20–25 minutes. Serve with grilled fish or roasted lamb.

Mashkoul
Rice with onion

Serves 5–6
2 cups (14 oz/440 g) basmati rice
6 cups (48 fl oz/1.5 L) cold water
1 tablespoon salt
¼ cup (2 oz/60 g) ghee or ¼ cup (2 fl oz/60 ml) vegetable oil
1 large yellow (brown) onion, finely chopped

Place rice in a fine-mesh sieve and rinse under cold running water until water runs clear. Drain well.

In a large saucepan, bring water to a boil then add rice and salt and return to a boil, stirring occasionally. Cook for 8 minutes, then immediately drain in a large sieve.

In a heavy saucepan over medium–low heat, heat ghee or oil. Add onion and fry until translucent, about 7 minutes. Raise heat to medium–high, and fry onion until crisp and lightly colored, about 7 minutes longer. Remove half of onion and ghee or butter to a small bowl and set aside.

Add rice to saucepan and toss with a fork to combine with onion. Put reserved onion on top of rice. Cover pan tightly and cook over low heat until rice is tender, 35–40 minutes. Fluff with a fork and serve piled on a platter. Mashkoul is a standard accompaniment to most Gulf States dishes.

Tabboulah
Bulgur and parsley salad

Serves 6–8

¾ cup (4 oz/125 g) fine bulgur (burghul)

2 cups (16 fl oz/500 ml) cold water

5 scallions (shallots/spring onions), finely chopped, including tender green tops

4 cups (6 oz/185 g) fresh flat-leaf (Italian) parsley, coarsely chopped

3 tablespoons fresh mint, finely chopped

¼ cup (2 fl oz/60 ml) olive oil

2 tablespoons lemon juice

1½ teaspoons salt

½ teaspoon black pepper, freshly ground

2 firm, ripe tomatoes

crisp romaine (cos) lettuce leaves

¼ cup (2 fl oz/60 ml) lemon juice mixed with ½ teaspoon salt

Place bulgur in a bowl and cover with cold water. Let soak for 15 minutes. Drain through a fine-mesh sieve, pressing with back of a spoon to extract moisture. Spread onto a kitchen towel to dry further.

Put bulgur in a bowl and add scallions. Squeeze mixture with hands so bulgur absorbs onion flavor. Stir parsley and mint into bulgur.

In a small bowl, beat olive oil with lemon juice. Stir in salt and pepper. Add to salad and toss well.

To peel tomatoes: place in a bowl, pour boiling water over, and let stand for 10 seconds. Drain, peel, remove seeds, then dice. Gently stir tomatoes into salad. Cover and chill for at least 1 hour before serving.

Serve in a shallow salad bowl lined with lettuce leaves. Serve lemon juice and salt mixture alongside, so it can be added according to individual taste.

Fattoush

Toasted bread salad

Serves 6
1 large pita bread
8 romaine (cos) lettuce leaves
   or 6 leaves of another variety
1 young green cucumber
   or ¼ English (hothouse) cucumber
2 medium tomatoes
1 cup (5 oz/150 g) green bell pepper
   (capsicum), chopped
5 scallions (shallots/spring onions),
   chopped, including tender green tops

6 tablespoons fresh flat-leaf (Italian)
   parsley, chopped
3 tablespoons fresh mint, chopped
DRESSING
1 clove garlic
1 teaspoon salt
½ cup (4 fl oz/125 ml) lemon juice
½ cup (4 fl oz/125 ml) olive oil
freshly ground black pepper

Toast pita bread until golden brown.
Break into small pieces or cut into
small squares using kitchen scissors.

Shred lettuce or break into small
pieces. Peel cucumber if desired,
quarter lengthwise and cut into
chunks. Cut tomatoes into small
cubes.

To make dressing: In a small bowl,
crush garlic with salt and mix to a
paste. Add lemon juice, olive oil and
pepper, then beat thoroughly with a
fork.

In a salad bowl, combine bread,
lettuce, cucumber, tomatoes, bell
pepper, scallions, parsley and mint.
Pour on dressing, toss well and serve.

Lubyi bi zayt
Green beans in oil

Serves 6
1 lb (500 g) green beans
¼ cup (2 fl oz/60 ml) olive oil
1 medium yellow (brown) onion, chopped
2 cloves garlic, chopped
1 cup (6 oz/185 g) tomatoes, peeled and chopped
1 tablespoon tomato paste
½ cup (4 fl oz/125 ml) water
½ teaspoon sugar
salt
freshly ground black pepper
2 tablespoons fresh flat-leaf (Italian) parsley, chopped

Trim beans and remove strings if necessary. Cut into 2-inch (5-cm) lengths or slit lengthwise.

In a frying pan over medium–low heat, heat olive oil. Add onion and fry until translucent, about 8 minutes. Stir in garlic and cook for a few seconds longer.

Stir in tomatoes, tomato paste, water, sugar, and salt and pepper to taste. Cover and simmer until tomatoes are soft, about 15 minutes.

Stir in beans and parsley, cover, and simmer until beans are tender, 15–20 minutes. Serve hot, or at room temperature as is traditional.

Fish and Seafood

Samak quwarmah
Fish curry

Serves 6
1½ lb (750 g) fish steaks or fillets
salt
2 tablespoons ghee or vegetable oil
2 medium yellow (brown) onions, chopped
1 teaspoon fresh ginger, peeled and grated
2 cloves garlic, crushed
½ teaspoon ground red chili
1 teaspoon Baharat (page 23)
1 teaspoon turmeric
1 cinnamon stick, about 1½ inches (4 cm) long
1 cup (6 oz/185 g) tomatoes, peeled and chopped
2 Loomi (dried lime page 22) or zest of ½ lemon
½ cup (4 fl oz/125 ml) water
Mashkoul (page 27) for serving

Rinse fish and pat dry with paper towels. Cut into serving sizes and sprinkle lightly with salt. Place on a plate, cover and set aside.

In a heavy frying pan over medium–low heat, heat ghee or oil. Add onion and cook until translucent, about 10 minutes. Add ginger, garlic, chili, Baharat, turmeric and cinnamon stick and cook, stirring, for 2 minutes.

Stir in tomatoes, Loomi (pierced twice with a skewer) or lemon zest, and water. Add salt to taste, cover and simmer for 15 minutes.

Place fish pieces in sauce, cover, and simmer until fish is cooked through, 15–20 minutes. Lift fish onto a platter with prepared Mashkoul. Remove Loomi or lemon zest and cinnamon stick from sauce and spoon sauce over fish. Serve hot.

Chebeh Rubyan
Shrimp balls

Serves 4–6

2 lb (1 kg) uncooked shrimp (prawns)
¼ cup fresh cilantro (coriander) leaves
½ teaspoon turmeric
½ teaspoon ground Loomi (dried lime page 22) or grated lemon zest.
¾ cup ground rice
1 teaspoon salt

FILLING

1 large onion, finely chopped
2 tablespoons ghee or butter
1 teaspoon Baharat (page 23)
½ teaspoon ground Loomi (dried lime page 22) or grated lemon zest

TAMARIND SAUCE

piece of tamarind the size of a small egg
2 cups (16 fl oz/ 500 ml) warm water
1 small onion, finely chopped
1 tablespoon ghee
1 large tomato, peeled and chopped
1 teaspoon Baharat (page 23)
¼–½ teaspoon ground chili
salt
2 teaspoons sugar

FOR SERVING

Muhammar (page 26)
cooked shrimp (prawns) and cilantro (coriander) sprigs for garnish

Shell and devein shrimp, rinse and dry well. Mix shrimp with cilantro leaves and put through food grinder with fine screen or process to a paste in food processor.

In a bowl, combine shrimp mixture with turmeric, ground Loomi or lemon zest and ground rice. Add salt and mix well with hand until thoroughly combined. Cover and refrigerate until required.

To make filling: In a pan, gently fry onion in ghee until translucent, stir in Baharat and Loomi or lemon zest and remove from heat. Keep aside.

To make sauce: Soak tamarind in 1 cup (8 fl oz/250 ml) warm water for 10 minutes and rub with fingers. Pass through a sieve, pressing pulp through with back of a spoon. Reserve tamarind liquid.

In a large, wide-based pot, gently fry chopped small onion in ghee until translucent. Add tamarind liquid, remaining 1 cup (16 fl oz/250 ml) water, tomato, Baharat, chili, salt to taste and sugar. Cover and simmer gently for 15–20 minutes.

While sauce is simmering, make Chebeh. Take about 1 tablespoon shrimp

paste and flatten in moistened palm. Place teaspoon of onion filling in center and close up, shaping into a ball. Keep hands moist during shaping. Repeat until ingredients are used.

Drop completed Chebeh into simmering sauce. Cover and simmer gently for 35–40 minutes. Chebeh will swell during cooking. Serve hot with Muhammar (page 26) and garnish with a few cooked shrimp and cilantro sprigs if desired.

Machbous al-gambari

Spiced shrimp and rice

Serves 4–5

2–3 tablespoons ghee or vegetable oil

2 cloves garlic, chopped

2 lb (1 kg) raw shrimp (prawns), shelled
and deveined

1 large yellow (brown) onion, chopped

2 teaspoons Baharat (page 23)

2 teaspoons turmeric

1½ cups (9 oz/280 g) tomatoes, peeled
and chopped

2 teaspoons salt

freshly ground black pepper

1 tablespoon fresh flat-leaf (Italian)
parsley, chopped

1 teaspoon fresh cilantro (coriander),
chopped

2½ cups (20 fl oz/625 ml) water

2 cups (14 oz/440 g) basmati rice

In a large pot over high heat, heat 1 tablespoon ghee or oil. Add garlic and
shrimp and cook, stirring frequently, until shrimp turn pink. Remove shrimp to a
plate and set aside.

Add remaining 1–2 tablespoons ghee or oil to pot and heat over medium–low
heat. Add onion and cook until translucent and lightly browned, about
8 minutes. Stir in Baharat and turmeric and cook for 1 minute.

Stir in tomatoes, salt, pepper to taste, parsley and cilantro. Bring to a boil and
add water. Cover and cook over medium heat for 5 minutes.

Place rice in a fine-mesh sieve and rinse under cold running water until water
runs clear. Stir into sauce and bring to a boil. Reduce heat to low, cover and
cook for 18 minutes.

Stir rice, then put shrimp on top of rice and gently stir through rice. Cover pot
and simmer over low heat for 3 minutes.

Stir rice again then remove from heat and let stand, covered, for 5 minutes.
Serve with pita bread, pickles and salad.

Samak mahshi
Fried stuffed fish

Serves 4–6
2 lb (1 kg) small, whole fish
salt
1 large onion, finely chopped
2 cloves garlic, finely chopped
2 tablespoons ghee or butter
1½ teaspoons Baharat (page 23)
½ teaspoon ground loomi (dried lime page 22) or grated lemon zest
½ teaspoon turmeric
oil or ghee for frying
flour for coating

Scale fish. Remove gills and clean out insides through small opening. Rub cavity with a wad of paper towelling dipped in salt to clean thoroughly. Rinse fish and dry well.

Fry onion and garlic in 2 tablespoons ghee until lightly browned. Stir in 1 teaspoon Baharat, Loomi or lemon zest and salt to taste. Remove from heat.

Stuff fish with onion mixture, placing a small wad of aluminum foil in opening to keep stuffing in.

In a small bowl, combine remaining ½ teaspoon Baharat with turmeric and 1 teaspoon salt and rub over fish. Set fish aside for 15 minutes to absorb flavors.

In a frying pan, heat oil or ghee. Coat fish lightly in flour and shallow fry in oil or ghee until cooked through. Drain on paper towels and serve hot, garnished with lemon and parsley.

NOTE Often curry powder is used instead of Baharat in Bahrain.

Chicken

Machbous ala dajaj
Spiced chicken and rice

Serves 4–5

2 large onions, chopped
2 tablespoons ghee or butter
1 tablespoon Baharat (page 23)
1 teaspoon turmeric
1 chicken, about 3 lb (1.5 kg), cut in
 pieces
1½ cups (9 oz/280 g) tomatoes,
 peeled and chopped
½ teaspoon powdered Loomi (dried
 lime page 22) or grated lemon zest

3 cloves
2 cinnamon sticks
6 cardamom pods
3 teaspoons salt
2½ cups (20 fl oz/625 ml) water
2 cups (14 oz/440 g) basmati rice
2 tablespoons fresh cilantro (coriander)
 leaves, chopped
2 tablespoons fresh parsley, chopped

In a deep, heavy pan, gently fry onion in ghee until translucent and beginning to brown. Stir in Baharat and turmeric and cook 2 minutes longer.

Add chicken pieces and turn in onion mixture over medium heat to brown lightly. Add tomatoes, Loomi or lemon zest, cloves, cinnamon, cardamom pods and salt, stirring well to combine.

Add water, cover and simmer over low heat for 20 minutes.

Place rice in a fine-mesh sieve and rinse under cold running water until water runs clear.

Stir rice gently into pot contents, add herbs and bring back to a slow simmer. Cover with lid and simmer on low heat until chicken is tender, stirring gently once or twice during cooking, 25–30 minutes. Remove from heat and let stand for 5 minutes.

Pile onto large platter with chicken pieces in center and serve hot with pickles, salad and pita bread.

Quwarmah ala dajaj
Curried chicken

Serves 5–6

1 chicken, about 3 lb (1.5 kg), cut in pieces
salt
1 1/2 teaspoons Baharat (page 19)
1 teaspoon turmeric
1/4 cup (2 oz/60 g) ghee
2 large onions, finely chopped
2 cloves garlic, crushed
1 teaspoon grated fresh ginger
1/4–1/2 teaspoon hot chili pepper
small piece cinnamon stick
1 cup (6 oz/185 g) tomatoes, chopped and peeled
2 Loomi (dried lime page 22) or thinly peeled lemon zest
3/4 cup (6 fl oz/180 g) water
FOR SERVING
Muhammar (page 26) or
Mashkoul (page 27)

Wipe chicken pieces dry and sprinkle with salt. Combine baharat and turmeric
and rub half of the mixture onto the chicken. Leave for 15 minutes.

Heat ghee in a heavy pan and brown chicken pieces on each side. Remove to
a plate.

Add onion to pan and fry gently until translucent. Add garlic, ginger,
remaining spice mixture, chili pepper to taste and cinnamon stick. Fry for
5 minutes, stirring often.

Add tomatoes, dried limes pierced twice with a skewer, or lemon rind, and
water. Add salt to taste and bring to a boil.

Add chicken pieces, reduce heat to low and cover pan tightly. Simmer very
gently for 1 hour until chicken is tender and sauce is thick.

Serve hot with Muhammar or Mashkoul.

Dajaj mahshi
Roasted stuffed chicken

Serves 6
1 chicken, about 3½ lb (1.75 kg)
¼ cup (2 fl oz/60 ml) melted butter
   or ghee
½ cup (4 fl oz/125 ml) water or
   chicken stock
RICE STUFFING
½ cup (3½ oz/105 g) basmati rice
¼ cup (2 oz/60 g) butter or ghee
1 small yellow (brown) onion, finely
   chopped

¼ cup (1½ oz/45 g) pine nuts or
   slivered blanched almonds
¼ cup (1 oz/30 g) chopped walnuts
¼ cup (1½ oz/45 g) golden raisins
   (sultanas)
½ teaspoon Baharat (page 23)
   or ground allspice
1 cup (8 fl oz/250 ml) water
salt
freshly ground black pepper

To make stuffing: Place rice in a fine-mesh sieve and rinse under cold running water until water runs clear. Drain well.

Melt butter or ghee in a saucepan over medium–low heat. Add onion and fry gently until translucent, about 7 minutes. Stir in pine nuts or almonds, walnuts and rice, and fry, stirring often, for 5 minutes.

Add raisins, Baharat or allspice, water and salt and pepper to taste. Stir well, cover and cook over low heat until water is absorbed, about 10 minutes. Remove from heat and let cool.

To make chicken: Preheat oven to 350°F (180°C/Gas 4). Rinse chicken and pat dry with paper towels. Fill cavity with rice stuffing, and truss. Rub chicken with salt and pepper.

Coat a baking dish (roasting pan) with some of melted butter or ghee. Put chicken in dish and baste with remaining butter or ghee. Add water or stock to dish. Roast chicken, basting often with liquid, until juices run clear when pierced at the thigh, about 1½–2 hours.

Spoon stuffing into center of a platter. Cut chicken into serving portions and arrange around stuffing.

Beef and Lamb

Basal mahshi
Stuffed onion

Serves 6–8

1 oz/30 g tamarind pulp

1 cup (8 fl oz/250 ml) warm water

5 large yellow (brown) onions, unpeeled

1½ lb (750 g) ground (minced) beef
or lamb

½ cup (3½ oz/105 g) long-grain rice,
rinsed

1½ teaspoons baharat (page 23)

½ teaspoon turmeric

salt

freshly ground black pepper

½ cup (3 oz/90 g) tomatoes, peeled
and chopped

2 tablespoons tomato paste

2 tablespoons fresh parsley, chopped

1 tablespoon vegetable oil

1 tablespoon melted ghee
or vegetable oil

2 teaspoons sugar

In a small bowl, soak tamarind in ½ cup (4 fl oz/125 ml) warm water for 30 minutes. Strain into a bowl, pressing with back of spoon to separate pulp from liquid. Reserve liquid and discard seeds and fibers.

Peel onions and carefully cut out root with the point of a knife. Slit onion on one side through to center, cutting from top to root end.

Bring a pot of water to a boil, add onions and boil until softened, 8–10 minutes. Drain and let cool.

In a bowl, thoroughly combine beef or lamb with rice, Baharat, turmeric, salt and pepper to taste, tomatoes, tomato paste, parsley and vegetable oil.

Carefully separate onion layers. Outer layers may be cut in half; leave inner layers intact. Discard onion centers. Place about 1 tablespoon meat mixture on a layer of onion and roll up firmly.

Coat a heavy saucepan with melted ghee or oil. Place onion rolls in pan with seam-side down. Sprinkle layers lightly with salt. Combine tamarind liquid with remaining ½ cup (4 fl oz/125 ml) warm water and sugar. Pour over rolls.

Invert a heavy plate on top of rolls to keep them in place during cooking. Cover, bring to a simmer over medium heat, reduce heat to low and cook for 1½ hours. Serve hot with salads, pickles and pita bread. The onions may also be served at room temperature as an appetizer.

Bamya bi lahim
Lamb with okra

Serves 5–6

2 lb (1 kg) boneless stewing lamb

5 tablespoons ghee, clarified butter or
olive oil

1 large yellow (brown) onion, finely
chopped

½ teaspoon ground cumin

1 cup (6 oz/185 g) tomatoes, peeled
and chopped

2 tablespoons tomato paste

½ cup (4 fl oz/125 ml) chicken or lamb
stock or water

salt

freshly ground black pepper

½ teaspoon sugar

1 lb (500 g) okra

3–4 cloves garlic, chopped

1 teaspoon ground coriander

pinch ground red chili

Preheat oven to 325°F (170°C/gas 3). Trim lamb and cut into 1¼-inch (3-cm)
cubes. In a heavy frying pan over high heat, heat 2 tablespoons ghee, butter or
oil. Add lamb in a single layer and brown on all sides. Transfer lamb to baking
dish (large casserole) as each batch browns.

Reduce heat to medium–low, add onion to pan and fry until translucent,
7 minutes. Add cumin, tomatoes, tomato paste and stock or water. Stir well to
lift browned bits from bottom of pan.

Pour tomato mixture over lamb in baking dish (large casserole). Season with
salt and pepper and add sugar. Cover tightly with lid or aluminum foil and bake
for 1½ hours.

Rinse okra and trim stems without cutting into pods. In a frying pan over
medium heat, heat 1 tablespoon ghee, butter or oil. Add okra and fry, tossing
gently, for 3 minutes. Arrange okra on top of lamb, cover, and cook until meat is
tender, about 30 minutes longer.

In a small bowl, crush garlic with ¼ teaspoon salt and mix to a paste. In a
small frying pan over medium–low heat, heat remaining 2 tablespoons ghee,
butter or oil. Add garlic and cook, stirring constantly, until golden. Do not allow
garlic to scorch. Remove from heat and stir in coriander and chili.

Pour hot garlic mixture over okra and lamb. Serve with boiled rice.

Lahim bi fakiha
Lamb with dried fruit

Serves 5–6

2 lb (1 kg) boneless lamb shoulder
¼ cup (2 oz/60 g) ghee or ¼ cup (2 fl oz/60 ml) vegetable oil
1 medium yellow (brown) onion, chopped
2 cups (16 fl oz/500 ml) water
salt
small piece cinnamon stick
1 Loomi (dried lime page 22) or lemon zest from ½ lemon
½ cup (3 oz/90 g) pitted dates, chopped
¾ cup (4 oz/125 g) dried apricots
¾ cup (4 oz/125 g) dried prunes, pitted
¼ cup (1½ oz/45 g) golden raisins (sultanas)
2 tablespoons brown sugar

Cut lamb into ¾-inch (2-cm) cubes. In a heavy saucepan over high heat, heat half of the ghee or oil. Add lamb and cook, turning as needed, until browned on all sides, 8–10 minutes.

Push meat to one side, add onion and cook for 5 minutes. Reduce heat to low and add 1 cup (8 fl oz/250 ml) water, salt to taste, cinnamon stick and Loomi (pierced twice with a skewer) or lemon zest. Cover and simmer 45 minutes.

Place chopped dates in a small pan with remaining 1 cup (8 fl oz/250 ml) water. Set over low heat until dates soften. Press through a sieve into a bowl to puree.

Add date puree, apricots, prunes, raisins and brown sugar to saucepan. Stir to combine, cover tightly and simmer until lamb is tender, about 1 hour. Add more water during this time if meat and fruit seem dry.

Remove cinnamon and Loomi or lemon zest and discard. Serve with boiled rice.

Tharyd

Braised meat and potatoes

Serves 5–6

2 lb (1 kg) boneless stewing lamb or beef

2 large onions, chopped

2 tablespoons ghee or vegetable oil

2 teaspoons Baharat (page 23)

1 clove garlic, crushed

2 cups (12 oz/ 370 g) tomatoes, peeled and chopped

¼ cup (2 oz/60 g) tomato paste

2 teaspoons salt

½ teaspoon freshly ground black pepper

¼ cup (1/4 oz/7 g) fresh parsley, chopped

1½ lb (750g) waxy potatoes

1 large pita bread

chopped fresh parsley for garnish

Trim meat and cut into cubes. In a heavy based pan gently fry onions in ghee or oil until transparent. Increase heat and add meat cubes. Stir until meat loses red colour, add spices and garlic and cook 1 minute. Add tomatoes, tomatoes paste, salt, pepper and parsley. Cover tightly and simmer very gently on a low heat for 1 hour.

Peel potatoes and halve if large. Add to pan, cover and simmer until meat and potatoes are tender, for further 1 hour. Add a little water if necessary during cooking to prevent meat sticking to base of pan.

Cut pita bread into small pieces and place in serving dish. Ladle meat, potatoes and sauce on top, and sprinkle with chopped parsley for garnish. Serve with salad and pickles.

Kabab bi laban

Lamb kebabs with yogurt marinade

Serves 5-6

1½ lb (750 g) boneless lamb shoulder
1 cup (8 oz/250 g) plain whole-milk
    yogurt
2 cloves garlic, crushed
1 teaspoon salt
freshly ground black pepper

3 large whole wheat (wholemeal) pita
    breads, split in half
sliced tomatoes
sliced yellow (brown) onions
lemon wedges for garnish
fresh cilantro (fresh coriander) sprigs
    for garnish

Cut lamb into 1¼-inch (3-cm) cubes.

In a glass or ceramic bowl, combine yogurt, garlic, salt and a generous grinding of pepper. Add lamb cubes, stir to coat, cover and refrigerate for 4–5 hours or overnight (up to 12 hours).

Prepare a fire in a grill (barbecue), preferably charcoal. Thread 5 or 6 cubes of lamb on each of 6 metal skewers, leaving a little space between cubes. Brush off excess marinade, leaving a thin film.

If possible, set skewers across sides of the grill (barbecue) so meat is not directly on grill rack. Grill kebabs, turning them frequently until cooked to medium, about 10 minutes.

Remove cubes from each skewer and place on a pita bread half. Add tomato and onion slices. Fold bread to keep meat warm and serve immediately, garnished with lemon wedges and cilantro sprigs.

Khouzi
Baked whole lamb

Serves 5–6

1 small lamb, 20–25 lb (10–12 kg)

salt

¼ cup Baharat (page 23)

2 teaspoons turmeric

1 small chicken, 2 lb (1 kg), optional

3 hard-cooked eggs, optional

½ cup (4 fl oz/125 ml) rosewater

2 teaspoons saffron threads, pounded

5 cups (2 lb/1 kg) basmati rice

1 cup (8 oz/250 g) ghee or butter

3 large onions, finely chopped

5 cups (40 fl oz/1.25 L) water

1 cup (5½ oz/170 g) blanched almonds
  or cashew nuts

½ cup (2½ oz/75 g) pine nuts

½ cup (2 oz/60 g) pistachio nuts

½ cup (3 oz/90 g) golden raisins
  (sultanas)

Wipe lamb inside and out with a damp cloth. Rub cavity and outer surface with salt, half of Baharat, and 1 teaspoon turmeric. Put aside.

If chicken is used, wipe dry with paper towels and rub cavity and skin with a little Baharat, turmeric and salt. Insert shelled hard-cooked eggs in chicken cavity. Set chicken aside until rice stuffing is ready.

In a bowl, put rosewater and saffron threads; let soak for 10 minutes. Place rice in a fine-mesh sieve and rinse under cold running water until water runs clear. Drain well.

In a large pot, melt ½ cup (4 oz/125 g) ghee and add chopped onions; fry gently until transparent, stir in remaining Baharat and turmeric and add rice. Stir for 5 minutes over medium heat, then add water and bring to a boil, stirring occasionally. Add salt to taste, reduce heat, cover and simmer over low heat for 10 minutes.

Add nuts and raisins and fold into rice. Sprinkle half of rosewater mixture over rice. Cover pan, remove from heat for 10 minutes until liquid is absorbed. Put some of rice mixture in chicken, filling loosely. Secure opening with poultry pins.

Sew up cavity of lamb halfway and leave thread hanging. Fill cavity with some of rice mixture, put chicken in if using and complete filling with remaining rice mixture. Finish sewing up cavity.

Place a large rack in a very large catering-size baking dish (roasting pan) and place lamb on rack. Brush lamb with remaining ghee. Cover dish with large sheets of aluminum foil, sealing joins with double folds. Press foil under edge of dish to seal completely.

Bake in a moderate oven (350°F/180°C/Gas Mark 4) for 2 hours. Baste lamb with juice in dish and pour remaining rose water mixture over lamb. Cover dish again, return to oven and bake until very tender, for a further 2–3 hours, basting twice more with dish juices. Remove foil 30 minutes before end of cooking.

Lift lamb onto a large platter, remove string and spoon stuffing on the platter, setting chicken (if used) on top of stuffing.

Lamb can be carved, but it is much more fun to break off very soft tender chunks of meat. Enjoy your feast and feel like a sheik!

Kebat al batatis wal burkul

Bulgur and potato cakes
with lamb and apricot filling

Serves 6
1 lb (500 g) potatoes
¾ cup (4 oz/125 g) fine bulgur
  (burghul)
¼ cup (1 oz/30 g) plain flour
1 egg
salt
freshly ground black pepper
oil for deep-frying
LAMB AND APRICOT FILLING
2 tablespoons ghee or oil
1 large onion, finely chopped
500 g (1 lb) lamb, finely ground
  (minced)
¼ cup (1½ oz/45 g) almonds, chopped
½ cup (3 oz/90 g) dried apricots,
  chopped
½ teaspoon Baharat (page 23), optional
salt
freshly ground black pepper
¼ cup (2 oz/ 60 ml) water

Scrub potatoes and boil in jackets until tender. Drain, remove skins and mash.

Place bulgur in a bowl and cover with 2 cups (8 oz/260 ml) cold water. Soak for 15 minutes and drain through a fine sieve, pressing with the back of a spoon to extract moisture.

In a bowl, place potatoes, burghul, flour, egg and salt and pepper to taste. Blend thoroughly to a paste and shape tablespoons of the mixture into balls with moistened hands.

To make filling: In a frying pan, heat ghee or oil then add onion and fry gently until translucent. Increase heat, add ground lamb and cook over high heat, stirring often, until lamb is crumbly and begins to brown. Reduce heat to low, stir in remaining filling ingredients, seasoning to taste with salt and pepper and adding water last. Cover and simmer for 10 minutes on low heat. Remove from heat and cool a little.

Flatten a ball of burghul and potato paste in palm of hand and place a generous teaspoon of filling in center. Close up paste and reshape into a ball, then flatten to a thick cake. Repeat with remaining ingredients.

Deep-fry 6 at a time in hot oil for 7–8 minutes, turning to brown evenly. Drain on paper towels and serve hot.

Desserts and Sweets

Samboosa bi tamer
Date crescents

Makes 30
2½ cups (12½ oz/390 g) all-purpose
  (plain) flour
¼ cup (2 fl oz/60 ml) melted butter
⅓ cup (3 fl oz/90 ml) milk
¼ cup (2 oz/60 g) granulated sugar

¼ cup (2 fl oz/60 ml) olive or
  walnut oil
confectioners' (icing) sugar, optional
DATE FILLING
8 oz (250 g) pitted dates
¼ cup (2 oz/60 g) butter
1 teaspoon rosewater

Sift flour into a bowl. Add butter and, using your fingers, rub into flour until evenly distributed.

In a small saucepan over low heat, warm milk and sugar, stirring until sugar is dissolved. Let cool to lukewarm. Pour milk into flour. Add oil and mix until a soft dough forms. Knead in bowl until smooth.

To make date filling: Chop dates and put in a saucepan with butter. Place over medium heat and stir until mixture is combined and pastelike in consistency. Remove from heat and stir in rosewater.

Preheat oven to 350°F (180°C/Gas 4) .

Roll out dough on a lightly floured work surface until ¼ inch (5 mm) thick. Use a 2-inch (5-cm) cookie cutter to cut dough into rounds.

Place 1 heaped teaspoon of date filling in center of each round. Fold dough over filling to form a crescent. Crimp edge using your fingers or press with tines of a fork to seal.

Place crescents on ungreased baking sheets and bake until lightly colored, 20–25 minutes. Let cool on sheets for 5 minutes, then place on a wire rack to cool completely. Alternatively, dust crescents with sifted confectioners' sugar while hot. Store crescents in a sealed container for up to 1 week.

Qahwat
Coffee

The coffee pot of this region is called a dallah. Usually made of brass, it has a bulbous body that tapers at the top, a long, pointed spout, a curved handle and a high-domed lid.

Pour 1½ cups (12 fl oz/375 ml) water into pot and add 6 lightly pounded cardamom pods. Add 3 tablespoons finely ground, dark roast coffee and stir well. Bring to a boil, then reduce heat to low and simmer, covered, for 20 minutes; the grounds will settle.

Half fill tiny, handleless, bowl-shaped cups. The coffee is served unsweetened and up to three cups are served; it is not considered good manners to have only one cup. If you do not want more coffee after the second cup, wiggle the cup, which should be held in your right hand.

Ghiraybah
Shortbread cookies

Makes 35–40
1 cup (8 oz/250 g) clarified butter or ghee
1 cup (8 oz/250 g) confectioners' (icing) sugar, sifted
2½ cups (12½ oz/390 g) all-purpose (plain) flour, sifted

Chill clarified butter if it is too soft. Put butter or ghee in a bowl and beat until light. Gradually add sugar, beating until mixture is very creamy and light.

Fold flour into butter mixture. Knead lightly in bowl until smooth. If kitchen is hot, chill dough in refrigerator for 1–2 hours.

Preheat oven to 325°F (170°C/Gas 3).

Roll pieces of dough into walnut-sized balls and place on ungreased baking sheets. Press a floured thumb into center of each ball to make a dimple and to flatten dough slightly.

Bake until cookies are very lightly colored and almost firm, 20–25 minutes. Let cool on baking sheets until firm. Remove and store in an airtight container. These cookies are delicate and must be handled carefully. They will keep for 1 week.

NOTE These cookies are sometimes topped with a blanched almond or pine nut instead of being dimpled; others are finished with a dusting of confectioners' (icing) sugar.

Al batheeth
Date sweetmeat

Makes 20
1 cup (5 oz/155 g) whole wheat (wholemeal) flour
¼ cup (2 oz/60 g) ghee or clarified butter
1 cardamom pod, bruised
1 cup (6 oz/185 g) pitted dates, chopped
½ teaspoon ground ginger
confectioners' (icing) sugar for serving

Place flour in a heavy-based pan and stir over medium heat until lightly browned—about 10 minutes.

While flour is browning, heat ghee or butter in a small pan with cardamom pod. Heat for 5 minutes and set aside.

Add dates to flour and heat for 2 minutes until dates feel soft. Stir constantly.

Remove cardamom pod from ghee and add ghee or butter and ginger to date mixture. Stir until ghee or butter is evenly distributed and remove from heat. Mixture will be crumbly. Set aside until cool enough to handle.

Take about 1 tablespoonful mixture at a time and knead in hands, tossing from one hand to the other. When mixture holds together squeeze into an oval shape, molding it smoothly. Place on a plate and set aside until cool.

Pack in airtight container. Serve dusted with confectioners' sugar.

Index

Pictured on page 2: Mutabbal (Eggplant and Tahini Puree), page 20
Pictured on page 4: Ghiraybah (Shortbread Cookies), page 60

This edition published in 2004 by
Parkway Publishing
Unit 3 Taylors Yard
67 Alderbrook Road
LONDON SW12 8AD

© Copyright 2004 text, photography and design: Lansdowne Publishing Pty Ltd, Sydney,
Australia, www.lansdownepublishing.com.au
CEO: Steven Morris, email: sales@lanspub.com.au

Text: Tess Mallos
Photographer and stylist (except page 35): Vicki Liley
Designer: Avril Makula
Production Manager: Sally Stokes
Project Co-ordinator: Kathleen Davidson

ISBN 1 898259 06 2

Set in Trade Gothic and Journal Text on QuarkXPress
Printed in Singapore by Tien Wah Press